SPEAKING AND PRAYING IN TONGUES

A Non-Negotiable Christian Necessity

Apostle Michael Dessalines

Speaking And Praying In Tongues
A Non-Negotiable Christian Necessity

Scriptures taken from the Holy Bible, New International Version®, NIV®. Copyright © 1973, 1978, 1984, 2011 by Biblica, Inc.™ Used by permission of Zondervan. All rights reserved worldwide. www.zondervan.com The "NIV" and "New International Version" are trademarks registered in the United States Patent and Trademark Office by Biblica, Inc.®

First Printing, 2023

ISBN: 979-8-9875777-9-0

Michael Dessalines
Living Water Church of Waterbury
Eglise Eau de Vie de Waterbury
214 Walnut Street
Waterbury CT 06704
Livingw214@gmail.com

"Apostle Michael Dessalines is a great writer. He writes with great inspiration and deep thought. This book is captivating and educating. The sentence structure, punctuation, spelling and readability are awesome".

By the Editor

DEDICATION

This book is wholly dedicated to Jesus Christ my Lord and Savior for his grace, to God the Father for his love, and to the Holy Spirit for his fellowship. To God alone be all the glory and all the honor and all the praise forever and ever amen!

ACKNOWLEDGEMENT

I thank my lovely wife Joceline Dessalines for her unwavering upkeep through and through in writing this book. My gratitude goes to my spiritual father Apostle Jean Dieudonne for his guidance from the conception to the birth of this work. I want to present a heartfelt thanks to the members of Living Water Church of Waterbury for their support. I thank Mrs. Aline Etienne for her steadfast encouragement in this endeavor, Lenzye Clotaire for the faithfulness she continually shows in her service to the Lord, Irina Cajuste and Garnel Etienne for their reliable support. I want to thank Mrs. Andrelle Cajuste for her relentless devotion in her service to the Lord. I am grateful to Rev. Leonce Alexis for his years of investments in me. I cannot forget my brothers: Jude and Pastor Eliezard Dessalines for their unconditional support. Finally, I thank Remesse Pierre, Pierrecine Mervil, and Clodine Clotaire for their twenty years of faithfulness and their outstanding support to the church and in realizing this project.

FOREWORD

Apostle Michael Dessalines is a knowledgeable servant of God whose foundation has been established on scripture and revelations of the Holy Spirit. One of his great attributes is the simplicity by which he relays information. He has the ability to make a difficult topic easy to understand. As my spiritual son, I've watched him build and equip a strong body of believers in Waterbury, Connecticut. The people within the congregation he pastors are not just "church-goers," but through his teachings, are individuals who have built a stable relationship with Jesus Christ.

For some, the gift of tongues is no longer needed today. For others, the gift of tongues is a part of their everyday prayer life. Regardless of a person's viewpoint, this gift has been given by God to believers (1 Corinthians 12:10-11). It helps to edify oneself (1 Corinthians 14:4) and to pray in accordance with the will of God (Romans 8:27). As you dive into this book, you will learn more about this unique gift and why it is useful to you today. I pray that by the grace of God and the leading of the Holy Spirit, this book will help you to receive revelations behind the gift of tongues that will help to increase your prayer life and unlock new levels of God's power.

God bless you.

Apostle Jean Dieudonne

CONTENTS

INTRODUCTION

My goal in writing this book is to bring clarity and understanding on the topic of 'speaking in tongues' so that the average believer in Jesus Christ will be equipped enough to operate with great confidence in the knowledge of the word of God as it relates to that matter. It is not pretended that this book will cover everything on the subject matter but it is my sincere prayer that what is discussed here will place the reader on a launching pad that will catapult him/her to not only further investigate this topic just like the Berean brothers had done in the book of Acts of the Apostles (Acts 17:11) but also to experience this truth for himself or herself. It is also my hope that many believers reading this book will be baptized with the Holy Spirit with the evidence of speaking in tongues through the simple, easy-to-understand instructions that will be laid out in this book.

If this book can accomplish these two objectives, the rigorous process of writing and getting it published will be worthwhile.

THE TRIGGER

It was a Sunday afternoon in late 2015 after our worship service. The children were running all over the place with great joy to cause the space to be as loud and distracting as it could be. In the midst of it all, a church member looked at me with a confusing smile in her eyes saying: "Pastor, I have something to tell you." I did not hesitate because those words had created a great sense of urgency in my soul. I invited her to meet me in the middle of the noise at the back of the church. At that time, we did not have office space available for that purpose.

As we sat down, she gave me that same smile and began to look at her fingers as if she was counting them. I wanted to ask her: "what is going on?" but as a trained chaplain, I refrained from saying anything while letting her know that she has my undivided attention. Then she started sobbing. Then she uttered those three words so quietly that I could barely hear: "I have cancer" and she turned her face away from me. Then she added: "It's on my right breast" as she was fighting to no avail to keep back tears in her eyes. Upon hearing those words, my heart dropped.

As her pain was going through me, I opened my mouth and said to her: "God will take care of it. God will take care of it. Don't worry. He has done it before and he will do it again." Then she started telling me that she has already seen a specialist and they are working on developing a treatment plan to tackle the issue at hand.

After the dismissal of this meeting, I had a million questions going through my head that I did not have answers for: "Why weren't you aware of this before it happened? What are you going to do about it? Do you still maintain the idea that God still heals?" Then it was brought to my remembrance of an old friend who was diagnosed with such a condition and did not make it after her both breasts were removed one after the other over a relatively short period. This scenario and the questions were being played in my mind over and over again to the point that fear and doubt started to creep in.

As I was pushing back to convince myself that God will take care of it, I was reminded of what is said about Jesus in Isaiah 53:5: "But He *was* wounded for our transgressions. *He was* bruised for our iniquities. The chastisement for our peace *was* upon Him, And by His stripes, we are healed." As I was meditating on those words, came the pointing question: "Why do you have to wait for the house to be on fire before having water ready?"

Then I looked back to make an evaluation of what I know in what the Bible says about healing. I read that upon commissioning his disciples to preach the gospel, Jesus enabled them with both authority and power to heal the sick among other things. One of the remarkable things that all the disciples had in common, I found, was the experience of speaking in tongues. Jesus promised that they were going to receive power after the Holy Spirit has come upon them. When the Holy Ghost had come upon them in the book of Acts of the Apostles, instead of receiving power as we would all perceive it to be, the disciples received the gift of speaking in tongues. It was obvious that the power Jesus promised to the disciples was encapsulated within the gift of speaking in tongues. After that, those guys went out to change the world. Then I concluded that speaking in tongues is the first place to start if one wants to experience the power of God and I was not wrong about it.

CHAPTER 1

BIBLICAL PROSPECTIVE ON SPEAKING AND PRAYING IN TONGUES

In many Christian circles, the average believer has just a broad understanding of the ministry of the Holy Spirit in his or her life. That systematic deficiency can range from innocent unawareness to deliberate choices made to ignore such a powerful teaching in the body of Jesus Christ. The teaching and practice of speaking in tongues, one of the gifts of the Holy Spirit, divide family members, churches, and denominations. While supported in some Christian circles, others label it as unnecessary for our days, unbiblical, or downright demonic.

This shows how far the church has drifted away from the teaching of Jesus Christ, Apostle Paul, and the twelve original apostles of Jesus Christ. What God has given to be a blessing to the church has appeared to have been one of the most disruptive concepts in Christian circles. To understand the enormousness of that problem, let someone start speaking in tongues in a church where it is not taught or encouraged and watch the reactions of the people there.

People have solid beliefs for or against speaking in tongues in every religious circle. That is why many avoid talking about it openly. However, speaking in tongues was a very important component in the launching of and the survival of the church of Jesus Christ. It was a consistent practice in the churches Apostle Paul and the other disciples had planted. Apostle Paul said to the church of Corinth one time that: *"I thank God that I speak in tongues more than all of you." (1 Corinthians 14:18).* That means the church was accustomed to speaking in tongues except that Apostle Paul was doing it more consistently than the members of the church. Jesus himself said that Speaking in tongues is one of the five signs that were going to accompany those who believe in him in Mark 16:17. Finally, Apostle Paul encouraged the believers in 1 Corinthians 14:39[b] this way: "… Forbid not to speak with tongues."

The question we ask ourselves is why is speaking in tongues so controversial and ignored in so many Christian circles and movements? Could that controversy possibly be one of the devices used by our adversary to keep the people of God from benefiting the graces that unequivocally come from such an experience?

Through the pages of your bible, we will explore the origin, teaching, controversies, and benefits of speaking in tongues. We will prove to you that this gift of the Holy Spirit is still valid in the church today. At the end of this book, you will be led in a simple activation prayer to experience the gift of speaking in tongues on your own. Your life can never be the same.

CHAPTER 2

MY ENCOUNTER WITH HOLY SPIRIT

I was in my second year in college in 1997 when it happened. I was by myself in my dormitory room after all the other students had left campus for the weekend. All of a sudden, as I was singing the praises of God, words started brewing in my mind and coming out of my mouth effortlessly. I decided to go along with it. As I was speaking them out, I became conscious that those words can be put together in a form of a new language. With that idea in mind, I started writing some of them down as fast as I could as they were coming through. Out of excitement, I said to myself that I will teach my family members and close friends this new language and we could use it as a coded way of communication for ourselves.

A few days into speaking those strange words, although I was super edified speaking them out, I discovered that I had no meaning for them. My tasks had increased now. I started to write them down along with the meanings that were conveyed to my spirit at that time. I reached a point where I could not keep up in documenting the words and their meanings because the time spent writing them down had hindered their flow in my spirit. I discovered as I went back to my writings that the same word written several times had different connotations. In other words, I found out that the same word carried different meanings when I compared them together.

I did not understand what was happening to me at that time. Then, I switched only to the utterance of those words as the flow was coming uninterrupted. I had stopped writing them down because it was too cumbersome to do so. The flow of the utterance then started to diminish slowly and sturdily as I made no effort whatsoever to keep at it. A few weeks later, it had stopped completely. It did not bother me at all as it was not something that I sought nor knew what it was. It was fifteen years later that I understood that it was how I got baptized with the Holy Spirit with the evidence of speaking in tongues.

CHAPTER 3

FOUNDATIONS OF SPEAKING AND PRAYING IN TONGUES

S peaking in tongues is one of the doctrines of the Bible even when the emphasis on its teaching in many Christian circles is neglected, discouraged, or even labeled outright demonic. As a consequence of that neglect, it becomes the object of a mystery that brings all kinds of confusing interpretations. The reader who is new to this topic is strongly encouraged to approach this book with an open mind as the word of God needs no defenders.

Speaking about doctrines, four principles must be met for any Biblical Doctrine to be established as such. I will elaborate on all of them as they relate to the topic of speaking in tongues which is one of the gifts of the Holy Spirit to the earthly church then, now, and beyond. Through a brief overview, I will prove to you beyond any reasonable doubt that speaking in tongues, one of the nine main gifts of the Holy Spirit, has met all four of these parameters as one of the doctrines of the Bible called Glossolalia; as such is worthy to be taught in the body of Jesus Christ like any other doctrine of the Bible.

For a biblical doctrine to be established, the following parameters must be met in full:

1. *It must find its origin in the Old Testament.*
2. *It must have been taught by Jesus himself.*
3. *It must have been practiced by the early church.*
4. *It must have supporting scriptures to back it up in the bible.*

Let us consider the first principle

The outpouring of the Holy Spirit onto the disciples in the upper room left some confused and some in awe. The concerns of the confusion were that it was out of the norm for a group of individuals to start drinking wine to the point that they became drunk at nine o'clock in the morning. That was out of line with what their culture had allowed. The people in awe were praising the Lord because something inside of them had told them that what they were hearing came from nowhere else but from God.

This experience is not too different from ours in today's age. Two individuals listen to the same teaching on the word of God at the same time. Each one received a different message from the same speaking at the same time. That shows both God and the devil are at work. If you think God is not at work, check on what the devil is doing because both God and the devil can't be silent at the same time.

It was at that juncture that Apostle Peter stood up to remind the listeners that they were witnessing history, the fulfillment of an Old Testament prophecy already made by prophet Joel in the following terms: *"And it shall come to pass afterward, that I will pour out my Spirit on all flesh; your sons and your daughters shall prophesy, your old men shall dream dreams, and your young men shall see visions"*. *(Joel 2:28)*

Apostle Peter went on to interpret the meaning of that prophecy in Acts 2:17 when he connected their ability to speak in tongues on the day of Pentecost after their baptism with the Holy Spirit to the fulfillment of what Prophet Joel had already prophesied about. Apostle Peter took it a notch higher to say that this experience is not limited to the Jews only but also all believers in Jesus Christ's present and future. That settles it. In other words, although no one in the Old Testament spoke in tongues, it was prophesied and fulfilled in the New Testament on the day of the Pentecost.

Then Peter added in no uncertain terms that *"The (above-mentioned) promise is for you (his contemporaries at that time) and your children (their descendants) and for all who are far off—for all whom the Lord our God will call."* In a nutshell, this statement encompasses every believer (Jews and gentiles) from all nations and generations of the earth who would accept and believe the call of God to repentance and acceptance of his son Jesus Christ as the only way to salvation. In other words, everyone who claims to have been called by God has automatically inherited that promise. All believers in Jesus Christ are eligible for the same experience of Acts 2:1-3 regardless of country of origin, race, ethnicity, social economic status, or denominational appurtenances. The Pentecostal experience is available to all believers in Jesus Christ. If you want it, it can be yours today.

Let us consider the second principle

Jesus himself mentioned speaking in tongues as one of the five signs that will follow those who believe in him. The full account is found in the Gospel of Mark 16:17-18 in the following terms: *"[17]And these signs shall follow them that believe; In my name shall they cast out devils (1); they shall speak with new tongues (2); [18] They shall take up serpents (3); and if they drink any deadly thing, it shall not hurt them (4); they shall lay hands on the sick, and they shall recover" (5).*

Jesus uttered that statement way before the outpouring of the Holy Spirit. In other words, the disciples had to look forward to that encounter with the Holy Spirit because Jesus promised it. Later on, we find the Apostles not only speaking in tongues but also leading others to do the same as well both Jews and Gentiles. It is noteworthy to say that Jesus himself did not speak in tongues for the simple reason that he had already ascended to heaven before such a gift was made available to man on earth. The second principle is been verified.

Let us consider the third principle

It was there in the upper room when the Holy Spirit came on the 120 disciples who gathered under Jesus' command in Acts 1:4-5. Later on, we find Peter and John laying hands on believers to administer the baptism of the Holy Spirit with the evidence of speaking in tongues. That aspect will be explored further in the later chapters. Apostle Paul, many years later, was doing the same thing while assigning the early church to do the same as well. In short, 'speaking in tongues' was a common practice in the early church and still stands. The third principle is hereby verified.

Let us consider the fourth principle

There is a wealth of biblical evidence supporting the teaching of speaking in tongues and its validity in the body of Jesus Christ today. Here are a few of them:

In Ephesians 6:18, we find the language "supplication in the spirit" that is the same as praying in tongues as part of the armors of God to the believers then, today, and beyond: " *praying always with all prayer and supplication in the Spirit (in tongues) being watchful to this end with all perseverance and supplication for all the saints.* In Ephesians 5: 19, Apostle Paul encouraged the believers to sing songs from the Spirit or singing in tongues in the following terms: *"speaking to one another with psalms, hymns, and songs from the Spirit. Sing and make music from your heart to the Lord"* as he explained in 1 Corinthians 14:15.

The early church members were the first practitioners of speaking in tongues. Jesus had commissioned them to teach the whole world what he had taught them and they did that every time the opportunities had presented to them. In the book of the Acts of the Apostles 2:4, we read the following: *"And they were all filled with the Holy Spirit and began to speak in other tongues as the Spirit gave them utterance..."*

The following six scriptures underscore in their own merits the irrefutable display of evidence of speaking in tongues among the believers. They also make the case for its validity then, now, and beyond. You will find them in your own Bible.

1. *1 Corinthians 12:28* And God has appointed in the church first apostles, second prophets, third teachers, then miracles, then gifts of healing, helping, administrating, and various kinds of tongues.
2. *1 Corinthians 14:22* Tongues, then, are a sign, not for believers but for unbelievers; prophecy, however, is not for unbelievers but for believers.
3. *1 Corinthians 14:4* The one who speaks in a tongue builds up himself, but the one who prophesies builds up the church.
4. *Jude 1:20* But you, beloved, building yourselves up in your most holy faith and praying in the Holy Spirit (Praying in tongues).
5. *1 Corinthians 12:10* To another the working of miracles, to another prophecy, to another the ability to distinguish between spirits, to another various kinds of tongues, to another the interpretation of tongues.
6. *Acts 19:6* And when Paul had laid his hands on them, the Holy Spirit came on them, and they began speaking in tongues and prophesying.

I just proved to you that all four of the parameters that are responsible for a biblical doctrine to be established are impeccably met in the case of speaking in tongues. We conclude that speaking in tongues, one of the nine main gifts of the Holy Spirit to the church is a well-established biblical doctrine known as Glossolalia. Its application in our day is a non-negotiable necessity that will be explored later in this book.

CHAPTER 4

JESUS AT THE CENTER

There are just a few examples in the Old Testament of people who were filled with the Holy Spirit. They were either political or religious figures. That matter has changed in the New Testament. It was John the Baptist who first introduced the revelation of baptism with the Holy Spirit in the New Testament. At that particular time, he attributed the administration of such baptism to Jesus. In a contentious interaction with those who wanted to disqualify his ministry, John denied that he was the Christ. He further said that Christ will baptize people with the Spirit and with Fire.

It is important to note that people who do not understand what you do in your respective ministry may launch inquiries upon inquiries, mostly not in an attempt to have an understanding of it but to discredit it. It was no different for John the Baptist, for Jesus, and for Apostle Paul, and I can guarantee you that you will not get a pass on it. The good news is that despite all snares, your ministry will stand if it is built on the unshakable, unbreakable foundation that is Jesus Christ.

John the Baptist said the following to the people who came to question him in Matthew 3:11 *"I am baptizing you with water as evidence of repentance, but the one who is coming after me is stronger than I am, and I am not worthy to carry his sandals. It is he who will baptize you with the Holy Spirit and fire"*

It can be seen that John did not let himself get intimidated by people who were going to use his words against him. He spelled out the truth as he knew it. Intimidation is one of the tools in the devil's arsenal used to reduce into quietness the most zealous believers in the cause of the gospel. It is also a tool that the most powerful use against the lesser to keep them under subjection. The truth of the matter is that the devil does not have all the resources it takes to keep fighting a believer through the means of intimidation forever. This is why the Bible teaches in James 4:7-8 to *"Submit yourselves therefore to God. Resist the devil, and he will flee from you."* If we resist the devil the right way, he will gather all his resources and invest them somewhere else where he can have better results. We ought to put up together a robust rebellion against the devil every day and we will see how fast the devil will run from us. Here again, *"Not by might nor by power, but by my Spirit,' says the LORD"* (Zachariah 4:1).

CHAPTER 5

THE PERSONALITY OF
THE HOLY SPIRIT

We know who Jesus is because he came walking on this earth just like us. We know who God the father is because we can all relate to a father figure in our lives and around us. We know that both of them are currently in heaven. That begs the following two questions: 1) Who is the Holy Spirit and 2) Where is he at the present moment? I am glad that you asked.

Who the Holy Spirit is

Jesus told us who the Holy Spirit is before he ascended to heaven. The Hebrew word that translates spirit or breath is 'Ruah'. It is a grammatically neutral noun that is rendered as 'it'. However, Jesus in his reference to the Holy Spirit used the same word 'Ruah' not as an 'it' but as a 'he'. Automatically, that tells us that the Holy Spirit is a person.

We know that the Holy Spirit shows all the characteristic traits of a person as it is reported to us in the Bible. He has an intellect according to 1 Corinthians 2:10-11. He has a will according to 1 Corinthians 2:11 and He has emotions according to Romans 15:30.

The Bible says that the Holy Spirit is the third person of the Godhead. Jesus identifies the Holy Spirit as our helper, our guide, our counselor, our comforter, and so forth. The Holy Spirit is also represented by a dove, water, fire, wind, and so forth. Nonetheless, the Holy Spirit is not a dove, water, fire, or wind. I want to underscore that the Holy Spirit is not a junior God due to his position as the Godhead. His divine nature is equally important as that of God the Father and God the son.

Where the Holy Spirit is

The Holy Spirit is the God whom many believers do not know well enough. The Holy Spirit lives inside of us. This is what Apostle Paul said in Ephesians 4:30 *"And do not grieve the Holy Spirit of God, with whom you were sealed for the day of redemption."*

In other words, the Lord God almighty lives inside of us. This is a guarantee that we have as believers in Jesus Christ. God is with us everywhere we are and is present in everything we do. God is a witness to everything we say, do, and go through and is forever present with us. That echoes Matthew 28:20 where Jesus said: *"... I am with you always..."*

The word of God teaches us that God the father provides a set of gifts to the church, God the son provides a set of gifts to the church, and God the Holy Spirit provides a set of gifts to the church as well. Our interest at this time has to do with the main gifts that the Holy Spirit provides to the church.

The Inauguration of the Church

In Acts 1:8, Jesus said that his disciples would receive power after the Holy Spirit would have come upon them. In Acts 2, we find 120 of the disciples in the upper room praying and waiting. That was ten days after Jesus had ascended to heaven and fifty days after he was resurrected from the dead. Instead of receiving what everyone would perceive to be power, the Holy Spirit distributed tongues of fire on the head of all attendants of that particular meeting. The truth is that the power of God was encapsulated in the tongues of fire provided by the Holy Spirit on that day.

CHAPTER 6

THREE BAPTISMS

In the line of this work, we are defining baptism as immersing someone completely in water. It is accomplished when every inch of the body is thoroughly covered with water. It can be physical and spiritual. The word of God mentions several types of baptisms. Three of them are closely related to the works of the Holy Spirit in the life of the believer. We will explore them very quickly to foster a better understanding of the role they play in the way they each correlate with the gift of speaking in tongues. They are baptism in Christ (1), Baptism in Water (2), and Baptism with the Holy Spirit (3).

1. Baptism in Christ:

This first baptism is mandatory and permanent as salvation is dependent upon it. It is performed by the Holy Spirit. In this process, the Holy Spirit baptizes the believer into Jesus Christ. The only participation of the believer is total consent. There are no apparent physical signs or manifestations following that baptism on the part of the believer. It is accepted by faith. Apostle Paul said to that effect in 1 Corinthians 12:12: *"For by one Spirit are we all baptized into one body (the body of Christ)..."* Furthermore, he said about the permanency of that baptism in Ephesians 4:30: *"And grieve not the Holy Spirit of God, whereby you are sealed unto the day of redemption."*

2. Baptism in water:

This is a direct order given to his disciples by Jesus Christ himself. Matthew 28:19 reports this direct order of Jesus in the following terms: *"Therefore go and make disciples of all nations, baptizing them in the name of the Father and of the Son and of the Holy Spirit"*. Apostle Paul further elaborates on it this way in Romans 6:3-4: *"Do you not know that all of us who have been baptized into Christ Jesus were baptized into his death? We were buried therefore with him by baptism into death, in order that, just as Christ was raised from the dead by the glory of the Father, we too might walk in newness of life"*. We receive that baptism following our conversion to Jesus Christ. The purpose of this baptism is to acknowledge Jesus before man. It is performed by man. This was the kind of baptism that John the Baptist was engaged in. That task was primarily assigned to him by God to enable him to identify the one who was to come to save the world: Jesus Christ.

3. Baptism with the Holy Spirit

The third baptism is after salvation. The Bible shows that it can come before or after the second one. It is not mandatory nonetheless it is of utmost importance in the life of the believer in Jesus Christ. This baptism is performed by Jesus Christ himself when he baptizes us (believers) with the Holy Spirit. This baptism does not save but allows the potential of the Holy Spirit who already indwells in us to come upon us to give us the enablement we need for ministry.

When we are converted to Jesus Christ, the Holy Spirit enters inside of us for our salvation. When we are baptized with the Holy Spirit, the Holy Spirit comes on or upon us for ministry.

This is what Jesus was talking about in Acts 1:4-5 when he told his disciples to tarry in Jerusalem until they were endued with the power from on high. In verse 8 of the same chapter, Jesus further explained what he meant in verses 4-5 in those terms: *"But you will receive power when (after) the Holy Spirit comes* on (upon) *you…"* The purpose of that baptism is to allow the Holy Spirit to come upon the believer with the power to do the works of the kingdom of God. This is referred to as the infilling with the Holy Spirit. This is something that the believer must seek after through daily conscientious efforts. We make these efforts through holy living and our fine tuning with the voice of God not to be saved once more but to be empowered for the works of ministry.

The baptism with the Holy Spirit is accomplished when the personality of the Holy Spirit is smeared and rubbed on the personality of the individual receiving that baptism. Many people experience God's power going through them like an electric current filling them with great joy and happiness during and after the baptism with the Holy Spirit.

The baptism with the Holy Spirit is a separate experience that comes after salvation. This is available to all believers but not all of them come to experience it. John the Baptist's prophecy on that particular baptism is reported in all four gospels highlighting its importance. He prophesied that Jesus was going to baptize his believers with the Holy Spirit. In two out of the four places, he added that Jesus was going to baptize his believers with the Holy Spirit and Fire. That is exactly what Jesus did in a two-step process. The first step of the process is found in John 20:23: *"As the Father has sent me, even so, I am sending you."* *And when he had said this, he breathed on them and said to them, "Receive the Holy Spirit..."* The second step of the process was completed in Acts 2:1-3 when the gift of tongues came upon the disciples in the form of fire in their meeting at the upper room on the day of Pentecost.

Evidence of the three baptisms together

Both Doctor Luke and Apostle John give highlights of the three baptisms: 1) In Christ, (2) In Water, and (3) with the Holy Spirit together this way: one in order and the other one indiscriminately.

Acts 2:38: "And Peter said to them, "Repent (1) and be baptized every one of you in the name of Jesus Christ (2) for the forgiveness of your sins, and you will receive the gift of the Holy Spirit (3)."

1 John 5:7–8 "For there are three that testify: the Spirit (3) and the water (2) and the blood (1); and these three agree."

"Repent" is the baptism unto salvation in Jesus Christ. "Be baptized in the name of Jesus Christ for the forgiveness of your sins" is the baptism in water. "Receive the gift of the Holy Spirit" is the baptism with the Holy Spirit.

In summary, baptism in Christ must be the first step before accessing the two other baptisms. The baptism in Water can happen irrespective of an established order. Some believers received baptism with the Holy Spirit after they received water baptism. That was the case for a few believers in Ephesus (Acts 19:2-7) while others received the baptism with the Holy Spirit and then were water baptized. For example, Saul, also called Paul, was first baptized with the Holy Spirit and then was Water baptized according to Acts 9:13-19. In any order, the Baptism in Jesus Christ comes first.

In the next chapter, we will discuss summarily the nine main all-time gifts that the Holy Spirit makes available to the body of Christ.

CHAPTER 7

THE NINE MAIN GIFTS OF THE HOLY SPIRIT

According to 1 Corinthians 12:1-11, the Holy Spirit gives nine gifts to the body of Jesus Christ. Due to their nature, those nine main gifts are grouped under three categories. Each category has a set of three gifts.

The first category called Revelatory gifts comprises the following three spiritual gifts:

1. Word of Knowledge

Through this gift, the Holy Spirit makes available past and present information about a person, an event, a place, and so forth that was otherwise unknown to the speaker.

In John 4:18, Jesus said to the Samaritan woman: *"For you have had five husbands, and you aren't even married to the man you're living with now"*. This word of knowledge caught that woman by surprise. As a result, she left where she was to tell others that she has found someone who told her all that she has ever done. It is good to note that whenever the Holy Spirit allows the manifestation of the word of knowledge, he never does it to embarrass nor to condemn but to redeem.

2. Word of Wisdom

This gift of the Holy Spirit enables a believer to speak on forthcoming events and things that would come to pass in a present, near, or far future.

Noah, for example, preached for 120 years the same message about a flood coming. When the time has come, what he said has come to pass. The word of God contains scores of the word of wisdom that have already been fulfilled and scores of others that are yet to come to pass. What God says will come to pass anyhow because the Bible says in Psalm 138:2 that God has exalted his word above his name.

3. Discerning of Spirits

This gift is an ability given by the Holy Spirit to identify what spirit is behind a person's action at a given time. That spirit can either be of God, of the devil, or the person posing the action.

In our first example, we find a fascinating account in the book of Acts 13:4-12 about a certain Jewish sorcerer and false prophet called Bar-Jesus also known as Elymas. Seeing his efforts in opposition to the Gospel being preached, filled with the Holy Spirit, Saul also known as Apostle Paul identified the spirit that was manipulating Elymas and rebuked him severely and the evil spirit left him.

A second example of the gift of discerning spirits in action is found in the Gospel of Luke 22:31. This is a very interesting one. Jesus made a statement about Peter. In the eyes of everyone, what Jesus had said had come to pass. First Jesus said to Peter in Luke 22:31: *"Simon, Simon, Satan has asked to sift each of you like wheat"*. Jesus automatically identified the spirit behind Peter's intervention in the prior verse. Note here that Satan had to ask for permission to sift Peter and the other disciples. This is a spiritual law. For any spirit to have an expression in the physical world that you and I currently live in, he has to secure a certain type of formal or non-formal permission either overtly or covertly. The sad thing is that Satan takes that permission very seriously regardless if it was obtained through joking or not, regardless of whether we meant it at the moment or not. *"*

A third example is found in the gospel of Matthew 16. In the conversation of knowing who people said Jesus was, Peter responded by saying that Jesus was the Christ, the son of the leaving God. Once more, Jesus immediately told us the spirit behind that statement in those words of Peter in verse 17: *"Blessed are you, Simon son of Jonah, for this was not revealed to you by flesh and blood, but by my Father in heaven."*

Our last example is one of the women possessed by the spirit of divination in the book of Acts of the Apostles 16. We see this gift of discerning of spirits at work when Apostle Peter accurately identified what was behind the seemingly non-harmful statements made by that woman saying in verse 17: *"These men are the servants of the most high God, which shew unto us the way of salvation"*. In Verse 18, the real reason why the woman was making that same statement over three days straight was finally revealed. *"...But Paul, being grieved, turned and said to the spirit, I command thee in the name of Jesus Christ to come out of her. And he (the evil spirit) came out the same hour."*

B. The second category called the Power Gifts comprises the following three spiritual gifts:

3. Gift of Faith

This is the enablement of the Holy Spirit to the believers to achieve what is impossible in ways that cannot be humanly explained. That way, the Holy Spirit uses humans as catalysts to facilitate what God is about to do. This is why no glory is to be attributed to man because man plays the role of a facilitator only.

The believers in the book of Acts of the Apostles Acts 4:30-31 put it at best in their following prayer to God: *"Stretch out your hand to heal and perform signs and wonders through the name of your holy servant*

Jesus. " In other words, when they would have stretched their hands, it would not have been theirs in reality but God's. This is the reason why all the credits go to God only.

In Daniel 6, we see the gift of faith in action before, during, and after Daniel was thrown into the lion's den. We also find the same attitude in Daniel 3:8-25 before, during, and after Shadrach, Meshach, and Abednego were thrown into the fiery furnace. In both cases, the actors were so confident that God was on their sides that not even their lives seemed to have mattered anymore when the divine prerogatives had crossed the path of their own. The result was that God showed up in ways that disabled men's ability to forget what had happened there. He accomplished through them exploits that were impossible for them to accomplish on their own.

In the New Testament, we see the gift of faith in action in the Gospel of Mk 4:35-41. It is in this account that Jesus rebuked the wind and the waves and suddenly, the sea became calm.

4. Gifts of Healing

This is the ability of the Holy Spirit given to a believer to minister various kinds of healing and health restoration.

Jesus did it. In Matthew 4:23-24, we read that: *"Jesus went throughout Galilee, teaching in their synagogues, proclaiming the good news of the kingdom, and healing every disease and sickness among the people. News about him spread all over Syria, and people brought to him all who were ill with various diseases, those suffering severe pain, the demon-possessed, those having seizures, and the paralyzed; and he healed them."*

His disciples did it in Luke 10:17: *"The seventy-two returned with joy and said, "Lord, even the demons submit to us in your name." In Acts 19:11-12 we read the following: [11] God did extraordinary miracles through the hands of Paul, [12] so that even handkerchiefs and aprons that had touched him were taken to the sick, and their illnesses were cured and the evil spirits left them". We are commissioned by Jesus to keep on doing it in Matthew 10:8 in the following way: "Heal the sick, cleanse the lepers, raise the dead, cast out devils: freely ye have received, freely give."*

I have seen this gift in action countless times in the Ministry of Apostle Jean Dieudonne and his wife Sheila Dieudonne, founders and overseers of the Demonstration Ministry in the State of Florida.

5. Gift of Working Miracles

The Holy Spirit enables a believer through the power and energy of God to cause something to happen in a way that interrupts the normal course of ordinary events.

The third category is called Inspirational gifts and it comprises the following three spiritual gifts:

6. Gift of Prophecy

Many times, the gift of the word of wisdom is mistaken for the gift of prophecy. As Dr. Lester Sumrall puts it, the gift of prophecy in the New Testament is *"A divine operation under the anointing of God designed to warn men and women of sin (or shortcomings) so that they might be ready when Jesus comes"*. That gift has a three-fold purpose in the body of Christ: Edification, Exhortation, and Comfort.

Although anyone enabled by the Holy Spirit can prophesy nonetheless, not everyone who can prophesy is a prophet. It is also noteworthy to say that preaching is not prophesying. By definition, to preach is to utter forth, proclaim or announce a message or simply to deliver a message or a sermon. On the contrary, prophecy as far as it relates to the New Testament, is to warn people against dangers to come through edification, exhortation, and comfort. Preaching can be anointed and inspired but is never supernatural while prophesying is a supernatural ability given by the Holy Spirit to the believer to warn others.

7. Diverse Kinds of Tongues

The reason why the Bible talks about diverse kinds of tongues is that there is a variety of tongues. The believer must be familiar with every one of them so that order can be established as Apostle Paul said it. Below are at least four kinds of them.

For our discussion here, I will put tongues in three categories, each one in its own merits: 1) A personal prayer language (1 Corinthians 14:15) 2) one that needs interpretation by either the person doing the speaking himself/herself or by another individual in the congregation (1 Corinthians 14:27). (3) One that the listener supernaturally receives the interpretation without aid while the speaker is unaware of the meaning of what he/she is saying (Acts 2:8). The last two are done in public while the first one is done in privacy.

a. Private Prayer Language

First, Apostle Paul talks about a kind of tongue that is the believer's private prayer language in 1 Corinthians 14:14. This language already has its residency in the life of every believer when Christ Jesus was accepted. It comes with being born again. Yes. It has already been rooted inside of you when you became born again. Whether you are using it or not that is what this discussion is going to be about. This is the kind of speaking in tongues that the believer does in private, away from the church or the believer's respective congregation. We can voluntarily turn on and off the switch of our private prayer language whenever we want to. It is the same as when we decide to pray according to our intelligence. It can be planned or spontaneous. It is just like praying with understanding in your native language whenever you decide there is a need to do so.

It is important to emphasize the fact that the Holy Spirit will give the utterance (word and sound) to any believer in Jesus Christ who is willing to initiate the process every time. Nonetheless, the Holy Spirit will never do the speaking for the believer.

b. Public Tongues Speaking

Second, Apostle Paul talks about a kind of speaking in tongues that can take place in a church setting. However, interpretation must be provided by either the person doing the speaking in tongues or by someone else in the congregation with the gift of interpretation of tongues. This must be activated by the Holy Spirit. Apostle Paul further said that it is forbidden to use the speaking in tongues in any church setting if an interpretation is not provided. The reason he provided is found in 1 Corinthians 14:22 where the Apostle said that speaking in tongues (in public) is a sign to the unbeliever. It is a message of love and of warning from God to the body of Jesus Christ. It is used to relay a specific message to the church. Someone can speak out loud and may be able to interpret the words that are coming out or may not be able to. In that second case, the Holy Spirit will appoint someone within the congregation to interpret what is being said through the gift of the Interpretation of tongues (Corinthians 12:11).

c. Native Language

A third kind of speaking in tongues is the one in which the Holy Spirit enables a believer to speak words just like the person is speaking an already existing tongue or dialect. When that happens, no interpretation is needed. The other party will hear the message in his or her native language in the absence of interpretation. The Holy Spirit supernaturally conveys what is being said to be heard and understood in the listener's own language. That was the experience of the people who came to Jerusalem to attend the Pentecost feast. They each heard the massage given by Apostle Peter in their respective language without interpretations as we see it happened in Acts 2:7-8.

8. Interpretation of Tongues

Apostle Paul talks about the gift of interpretation of tongues which is different from translation. In other words, the Holy Spirit can enable a believer in a congregation to not translate but to interpret or provide a prophetic explanation of the kind of tongues being spoken during a church service.

The above-mentioned three kinds of speaking in tongues are not to be confused with each other because this is where most misunderstandings happen in the body of Jesus Christ as they relate to speaking and praying in tongues.

The interpretation is different from the translation. Again, the purpose of the interpretation is to provide the key message, the general idea of the content of a message spoken in tongues. Translation on the contrary is to render a message into a different language word for word in a grammatically ordered way. This is not what we are talking about here. A long message in tongues may be short in interpretation as the Holy Spirit is conveying the core of the message to the target audience.

In summary, those gifts are still valid in the body of Jesus Christ until his return because no passages in the Bible from Genesis to Revelations have ever indicated otherwise. Anything stated, on the contrary, is men's personal opinion at its best.

Zeroing In

The focus of this work will be on the last of the three gifts of the Holy Spirit in the category of Inspirational gifts, more precisely the gift of speaking in tongues. Every one of those nine main gifts is relational. In other words, one must first have a saving relationship with Jesus Christ and second, one must be baptized with the Holy Spirit to become a candidate for either one or several of them to function under the anointing of the Holy Spirit.

The Baptism with the Holy Spirit precedes the activation of speaking in tongues. That is to say, a believer must be baptized with the Holy Spirit to receive the spiritual ability to speak in tongues. Throughout the New Testament, scripture establishes clear patterns to follow to attain that level of spiritual maturity.

The baptism with the Holy Spirit highlights some important characteristics in the life of the believer including but not limited to boldness, service, witnessing, and warfare.

Boldness

One of the hallmarks of the baptism with the Holy Spirit is that it brings a level of boldness that is incomparable in the life of its recipient. Let's take for example the eleven disciples of Jesus. Out of fear for their lives, they all scattered and deserted Jesus at his arrest. Peter denied knowing him at a time it mattered the most to stand up for Jesus. After their baptism with the Holy Spirit, all of them but one (John) died as proud and bold martyrs in some way for the cause of the gospel of Jesus Christ. Peter has become so bold that being beaten and threaten to be killed for Jesus did not intimidate him a bit after his baptism with the Holy Spirit.

Saul was persecuting the believers of Jesus Christ throughout his region. Following his conversion to Jesus Christ and his receipt of the baptism with the Holy Spirit through Ananias, in the book of Acts of the Apostles 9:10-21, Paul joined those same believers who were skeptical of him at first. His life was threatened so many times in so many ways. He was stoned and left to die. In a particular instance, his fellow believers had to smuggle him out of the city in a basket to avoid detection. That was the only way that his life could have been spared for the gospel of Jesus Christ. Saul did not take a vacation after that serious threat to his life. He did not tender his letter of resignation. He continued straight through his ministry in spreading the Gospel of Jesus Christ. He was eventually beheaded for the same cause that he previously stood against so boldly. In other words, his boldness has changed hands.

The baptism with the Holy Spirit brings a level of boldness that is beyond one's comprehension. The cold becomes hot for Jesus Christ. The thief gets right with God. The shy becomes brave. At a time when in many religious circles, the lukewarm attitude in the church is tolerated and even accepted, the boldness brought by the baptism with the Holy Spirit can turn our culture upside down for all the better reasons.

31

Service

Everyone who was baptized with the Holy Spirit in the New Testament examples also received evidence of speaking in tongues at the same time. There were no exceptions. This is not to be compared with some believers who were not baptized with the Holy Spirit. In the case of Ephesus, the believers had never heard about the existence or ministry of the Holy Spirit. Apostle Paul corrected that discrepancy and laid hands on them and they received the baptism with the Holy Spirit with the evidence of speaking in tongues. In the case of Samaria, baptism with the Holy Spirit was not administered to the believers there. Peter and John were dispatched from Jerusalem to Samaria to correct that discrepancy. They laid hands on the believers who received their baptism with the Holy Spirit with the evidence of speaking in tongues at the same time.

Following those two examples, we need to note that the believer in Jesus Christ receives the ability to speak in tongues at the moment of his or her baptism with the Holy Spirit. It should not be an expectation that it may happen at some point in the future. It can happen right then and there provided that the following two conditions are met: 1) The baptism with the Holy Spirit is properly taught and 2) There is a demonstration of faith on the part of the recipient to speak it out as the Holy Spirit gives utterance (word, sound). It is that simple. Jesus commanded the disciples to wait for that baptism so that we don't have to.

In summary, the three keys that unlock the spiritual gift of speaking in tongues are 1) conversion to Jesus Christ 2) Sound teaching on the subject matter, and 3) Demonstration of one's faith to appropriate oneself with that gift of the Holy Spirit by speaking it out.

Witnessing

Here is what Jesus said to his disciples in Acts 1:8 (NLT): *"But you will receive power when the Holy Spirit comes upon you. And you will be my witnesses, telling people about me everywhere—in Jerusalem, throughout Judea, in Samaria, and to the ends of the earth."* In other words, the believer in Jesus Christ is living with the mandate of witnessing or telling people about Jesus Christ everywhere. This task becomes easier after he or she has been baptized with the Holy Spirit and has received the power from on high.

As mentioned earlier, the disciples displayed the power of God wherever they went to tell people about Jesus Christ. In Acts 10:39, Jesus was anointed with both power and the Holy Spirit. Jesus turned around and made the same experience available to all who believe in him. In other words, Jesus enables the believer to do everything that he did and beyond. In the process of witnessing, the disciples cast out demons just like Jesus Christ did. They raised the dead just like Jesus Christ did. They healed the sick just like Jesus Christ did. Wherever they went, they managed to put up robust rebellions against the kingdom of darkness. In some places, they were hated for doing that. In some other places, they were loved for doing that. There were just recipients of the Holy Spirit and the Power that they received when they got baptized with the Holy Spirit. What is encouraging about this is that as Apostle Peter said: *"For the promise is for you and your children and for all who are far away, as many as the Lord our God will call to Himself." (Acts 2:39).* This is not limited to a certain ethnic group but to all believers in Jesus Christ everywhere regardless of their socio-economic backgrounds. That includes both you and me.

Warfare

One night, the Lord opened my spiritual eyes into the spirit realm and I saw what I was not prepared for. The whole experience took about fifteen minutes but will stay with me for the rest of my life. I did not start sleeping for long before I saw myself on a familiar street where there was no one except myself walking. All of the sudden, the whole scenery had changed. While I was on the same street, I felt like stepping over things that were slippery and my feet were being covered with things to cement them to keep me from moving forward. When I looked down, I noticed that the ground where I stood was filled with living human skeletons. The bones were still attached. The human form was there but there was no flesh on the bones. The strange thing about it was they were all crying in great agony as they were attached to one another like the links of a chain. I saw that every inch of the street was occupied by those human skeletons from one side to another. I could hear their voices of torment. They were not expressed in any human language but I fully understood them. Everywhere I place my feet, a company of those skeletons was trying to pull me down so that they can find something to stand on. The walk was extremely slow and terrifying for me. I had fought and fought like a soldier to stay afloat until I was transported by an unseen hand to a different place.

I am saying this to remind you that every battle we ever engage in whether willingly or unwillingly, overtly or covertly, originates from the spirit realm. Who knows the spirit real better than the Holy Spirit? That is why we need to have him show us the strategies of the enemy so that we can defeat the enemy every time and be victorious through Jesus Christ.

Every believer as far as the Bible is concerned is a soldier (2 Timothy 2:3-4) and is called upon to get engaged in daily spiritual warfare. In this war, the soul of man is at stake and the enemy is constantly using oppression, affliction, temptation, seduction, and deception as tools to destroy souls on one hand. On the other hand, through the power of the Holy Spirit, God provides encouragement, guidance, strength, protection, and enablement to win souls from the enemy. The use of righteousness as a weapon guarantees protection against the fiery darts of the enemy. The proper use of the blood of Jesus Christ guarantees victory every time. The believer must be aware that he is up against an enemy that will not stop until he incapacitates the believer through death, sickness, and attacks of all sorts. The enemy knows that he is already defeated by the blood of Jesus Christ but will make every last-ditch effort to inflict as much damage as he can before he finally goes down. What is more damaging than to be defeated by an opponent that was already defeated at the cross by the blood of Jesus?

We are enabled by the Holy Spirit to stand firm against the attacks of the enemy knowing if we resist the enemy with firm faith, he will flee. We are enabled by the Holy Spirit to war against anything that disrupts the original order of the creation in our lives and around us. In Luke 10:19-21 (KJV) Jesus said what follows: *"Behold, I give unto you power to tread on serpents and scorpions, and over all the power of the enemy: and nothing shall by any means hurt you"*. In other words, we are better equipped than the launching pads that hold the most powerful nuclear weapons in this world. We are equipped to inflict everlasting blows on the enemy daily. All it takes is to be aware of who we are in Jesus Christ.

A complete list of weapons needed to win the daily warfare can be found in Ephesians 6:10-18 and they are listed as follows: Truth, Righteousness, The gospel of peace, the helmet (hat) of salvation, and the sword of the Spirit, which is the word of God and praying in the Spirit (praying in tongues). The believer is guaranteed of winning every time that one or a combination of those weapons is used against the enemy. Furthermore, Jesus backs it up with the following statement that should boost our confidence in the battle: *"Truly I tell you, whatever you bind on earth will be bound in heaven, and whatever you loose on earth will be loosed in heaven." (Matthew 18:18)*. In short, both the loser and the winner of this warfare have already been determined. Jesus is the winner and the devil is the loser. Nothing can ever change that either on earth or in heaven and the believer is more than a conqueror through the blood of Jesus.

CHAPTER 8

BACK TO THE BASICS

During one of our Wednesday night Bible studies, a retired Baptist pastor visited us. It happened that we were discussing the gift of speaking in tongues as a result of being baptized with the Holy Spirit. During our Q&A session, the pastor said the following: "Many of us have been in church all our lives and we have never gotten as deep as you have today in this topic. Not because I deny this teaching is biblical but I just don't see the point of bringing it up now to the church at all because almost no one speaks about it". That statement shows the great need in our denominational circles to embrace the full teaching of the word of God even if it means something we were not accustomed to.

It is indicated in the Bible that someone may be saved and yet have the gift of speaking in tongues inactivated in his or her life. It doesn't mean that the individual is not a follower of Jesus Christ. It simply means that the believer needs to get baptized with the Holy Spirit with evidence of speaking in tongues. Shortly we will demonstrate this by showing you three clear examples of what happened in that regard to three groups of people in the Bible who were already believers in Jesus Christ.

Lack of Understanding in the Early Church

Again, let us emphasize the fact that in the book of the Acts of the Apostles, we read several accounts that demonstrate the experience of salvation and the baptism with the Holy Spirit with the evidence of speaking in tongues being two separate experiences. It is of utmost importance to reiterate the fact that speaking in tongues is not a hallmark of salvation. It is however a powerful tool to enable the believer to fulfill the purpose of his or her calling on this earth. This is a great encouragement to those who have been believers in Jesus Christ for a long time but had never experienced the gift of speaking in tongues as one of the nine main gifts of the Holy Spirit to believers of Jesus Christ.

Our first example takes us to the book of Acts 18:24-28. This is a report about a very well-known, educated, and well-versed man in the knowledge of Jesus Christ called Apollos. In this passage, he was teaching in Ephesus with great boldness in the synagogues about Jesus Christ with great accuracy. However, he knew only about the baptism of John. In other words, his teaching was limited only to the baptism in the name of Jesus leaving behind the baptism with the Holy Spirit. As a speaker myself, I could only imagine how sincerely and yet incompletely bold he was in his teachings. Following his presentation, Priscilla and her husband Aquila invited him over to their home and they expounded to him the way of God more adequately. It appears that Apollos had acknowledged his deficiency in the area of the baptism of the Holy Spirit and had gladly accepted the correction provided to him by the godly couple. Then he departed for Achaia with the encouragement and letter of support from the believers in Ephesus to minister there. Here again, we find a sincerely well-educated man of God lacking the knowledge and the understanding of baptism with the Holy Spirit. It took a God-loving couple to help fix that discrepancy.

Acts 19:1-7 contains our second example. It was there in Ephesus that Paul administered a quick verbal questionnaire to some disciples (of Jesus Christ). The answer he found was very captivating. Paul asked them the following simple question: *"Did you receive the Holy Spirit when you believed"?* This simple question of the Apostle points directly to the fact that salvation and baptism with the Holy Spirit with the evidence of speaking in tongues are two separate experiences. *"Did you receive the (baptism of the) Holy Spirit when you believed (for Salvation)?"* The disciples were very frank and honest in their answers to him by stating unambiguously that they were not even aware of the existence of someone called the Holy Spirit. This answer called for the subsequent follow-up question by the Apostle: *"In what name then were you baptized?"* They answered that they received the baptism of John. Then Apostle Paul taught them the right way and then administered water baptism to them in the proper way. Following that, he laid hands on them and they received the baptism of the Holy Spirit with evidence of speaking in tongues at the same moment.

Those individuals had already believed in Jesus Christ but they did not as of yet experienced baptism with the Holy Spirit. What was missing in their experience with Jesus Christ was the baptism with the Holy Spirit. As they opened themselves up to it, they received it and it is believed that their lives were never the same again. That was the cornerstone that shortly after gave birth to the Ephesus church.

Our third example is found in Acts of the Apostles 8:14-25. There, we read the account of Philip who was entrusted with the privilege of preaching the good news of the Gospel in Samaria. The evangelist was inspired by God to preach the gospel and at the same time to perform miracles, signs, and wonders. The choice was very clear for the natives who did not waste time in turning their backs on their favorite magician called Simon towards embracing Philipp's message. Then, Peter and John were sent from Jerusalem to Samaria with the purpose of baptizing the believers of Samaria with the Holy Spirit after they have believed. When they got on the ground, the purpose of their mission found meaning in the fact that the believers there were not baptized with the Holy Spirit. As good emissaries, they baptized them with the Holy Spirit and the believers received also the evidence of speaking in tongues. Then Simon, the unemployed magician, offered to purchase from Peter and John the copyright of the power he saw exhibited in the lives of those who were baptized with the Holy Spirit. That right was categorically refused to him because it belongs only to the Holy Spirit with a stern warning that he seemed to have taken very seriously.

Our bonus example is a direct response to those who still believe that speaking in tongues was made available only to the Jews. This account will show that this gift is also available to both Jews and Gentiles. It is found in the book of Acts 10. The reading of the whole chapter is recommended but the focus here is from verses 44 through 48. This time, God himself orchestrated Peter's travel to the house of Cornelius, a non-believer, a gentile. As Peter was sharing the Good News about Jesus Christ with this notable personality along with members of his family, the Holy Spirit descended upon them with the evidence of speaking in tongues, just like that. That experience was so remarkable that Peter once more had to explain himself this time to his fellow circumcised apostles in Judea as to why he dared enter the home of a gentile to minister. After he provided the background information as to how he ended up going there, Peter responded to his critics in those terms in Acts 11:17 *"So if God gave them (gentiles) the same gift he gave us (Jews) who believed in the Lord Jesus Christ, who was I to think that I could stand in God's way?"* That statement alone settled the matter.

This is a powerful reminder that a witness has a lot of explaining to do. That was the case for Moses. After witnessing what had happened in the burning bush, he had to explain it to others. Here Peter, after seeing what had happened, had to explain it to others who were, in that case, very judgmental of his decision to go to Cornelius' house in the first place.

This is in line with what the Bible says in 1 Peter 3:15-16: [15] *" But in your hearts revere Christ as Lord. Always be prepared to give an answer to everyone who asks you to give the reason for the hope that you have. But do this with gentleness and respect,* [16]*keeping a clear conscience, so that those who slander you may be put to shame by your good behavior in Christ."*

Again, one of the things witnesses do is to explain what they have seen, heard, and experienced. Even when the auditor is not interested in the facts being laid out he/she still deserves to hear them. What they do with them is their responsibility, not the witnesses.'

In summary, each of the four examples above shows the discrepancy in the knowledge of the baptism with the Holy Spirit with the evidence of speaking in tongues in various circles of believers. What is the most striking in all of it is the desire of the people involved to accept and embrace the teaching on the subject matter and move to receive it by faith. The believers in Samaria, Cornelius, Apollos, and the disciples in Ephesus experienced baptism with the Holy Spirit because they were open to it. Those examples together show how God had sent someone to help bring light to that important matter. If you have not yet experienced the baptism with Holy Spirit with the evidence of speaking in tongues, are you open to it? It can surely revolutionize your spiritual life for the better and it can start today.

CHAPTER 9

HEALTH BENEFITS OF
SPEAKING
AND PRAYING IN TONGUES

Praying in tongues generates many benefits that we generally put in two main categories: Health Benefits and Spiritual Benefits. This chapter is dedicated to addressing the health benefits of speaking in tongues while the next chapter is dedicated to addressing the spiritual benefits of speaking in tongues.

Health Benefits

According to a survey funded by the Bill and Melinda Gates Foundation, 95% of people in the world have some sort of health issue in some way. It means that only 5% of the people in the world have no health problems. To boost their immune system, almost half of the American population takes multivitamins regularly. That is a total estimated price tag of $30 billion every year.

Speaking in tongues has major positive health impacts on the lives of those who practice it constantly. In 2013, a Pew Research study found that only 18% of Americans were actively speaking in tongues at least several times a year. Nonetheless, science confirms better health outcomes among those who speak in tongues regularly as compared to those who don't. Dr. Andrew Newberg, through the Neuroscience Department in the Medicinal school at the University of Pennsylvania, conducted a study in 2006 on that subject matter. The findings of that study showed that people who speak in tongues rarely suffer from mental problems (like depression and stress). They were found to have been more emotionally stable than those who don't speak in tongues.

We just want to put the epidemiology of mental health issues into perspective in our society today. In the year 2020, a research study conducted by the National Institute of Mental Health found almost one in every five American adults was dealing with some sort of mental disorder. That finding was the same across all ethnic lines. It is noteworthy to underline that the findings pointed out that disparity in care has significantly impacted the severity of mental disorders within the ethnic lines.

Another major study conducted by National Alliance on Mental Illness in 2020 found that people who were constantly depressed were 40% more likely to develop heart diseases and metabolic problems as well when compared to people who were not depressed. It was also found that nearly 90% of people who killed themselves may have in some ways experienced symptoms of mental health issues. Due to the magnitude of the mental health issues in our society, in 2022 the US Congress allocated a total financial package of $1.5 Trillion to tackle it. This is a very serious issue that is taking our society and the world by storm and cannot be ignored.

The finding by the University of Pennsylvania that people who spoke in tongues tend to be more emotionally stable than those who did not speak in tongues and that the ones who spoke in tongues rarely suffered mental health problems shows that a relationship with God through Jesus by the power of the Holy Spirit not only saves souls but the body as well.

Furthermore, according to Huff Post Religion, praying in tongues helps senior citizens cope better with illnesses and live longer when compared with the ones who did not pray in tongues at all.

Dr. Carl Peterson of the Oral Roberts University in Tulsa, Oklahoma is a brain specialist. He conducted a research study on the relationship between the brain and speaking in tongues. He found that when people spend expended time praying in tongues and worshiping in the spirit (in tongues), there is an activity that begins to take place in the brain. The brain begins to release chemical secretions that entered the human immune system. Dr. Peterson found that the hormone released from the brain increases the body's general immunity. He further identified that when the hypothalamus gland located in our brain is stimulated, it produces the hormones responsible for that activity. In light of all those studies, the conclusion is that praying and worshiping in tongues promote physical healing and better health outcome.

Scientific support

Science had proven true what the word of God had said thousands of years ago. It is good that science aligned itself with the word of God but it is not an obligation because I believe the word of God infinite times over what science is proposing on any given day or time. Apostle Paul was inspired by the Holy Spirit when he communicated the following spiritual truth to the Corinthian Church in these terms: *"For if I pray in an unknown tongue, my spirit prays, but my understanding is unfruitful" (1 Corinthians 14:14).*

A study conducted by one of the most prestigious brain institutions in the United States of America confirmed unequivocally what the Bible had already said thousands of years ago. The study participants were asked to pray according to their intelligence as the imaging of their brain activities was being recorded. Then, they were asked to switch from praying according to their intelligence to praying in the spirit also known as praying in tongues as the imaging of their brain activities was being recorded.

The findings were very fascinating. It was shown that when the study participants were praying according to their intelligence, there were lots of activities in the frontal lobes of their brain suggesting a high level of brain activities. It was also shown that brain activities in the same areas were significantly lower when the participants switched to praying in tongues. In other words, the activity of using the same amount of energy to speak in tongues by-passes the brain's ability to understand what is being said. That is why it is not given to us to even understand what we are saying in our prayers without the express enablement of the Holy Spirit to interpret it.

CHAPTER 10

SPIRITUAL BENEFITS OF SPEAKING AND PRAYING IN TONGUES

Praying in tongues is also praying in the spirit. This spiritual discipline has countless spiritual benefits for those who practice it. Your Bible elaborates clearly on those benefits.

1. - Self-Edification

Jude strongly encouraged his New Testament readers to pray in the Holy Spirit (in tongues) to edify themselves. In other words, as a believer prays in tongues, he or she is building himself up on the foundation already laid down by Jesus himself block by block. This is a direct attack against situations and circumstances that aim at derailing our standing with God. Not doing so regularly is leaving unattended wholes that the enemy is trying to poke into our lives every day to grow larger with more devastating consequences. In Jude 10, we read the following: *"But you, beloved, building yourselves up on your most holy faith, praying in the Holy Spirit"*. This is a direct invitation to all believers in Jesus Christ, regardless of their Christian denominational appurtenances to adorn themselves in a daily self-edification process.

Apostle Paul takes it to another level when he bluntly stated that he who speaks in a tongue edifies himself (**1 Corinthians 14:4**). Life circumstances can cause sporadic instabilities, aiming at making them permanent, in our Christian walk. The work of self-edification is desperately needed to resist and push back against the attacks of the enemy that is not to be ignored in any way shape or form.

2. - Receipt of supernatural help

It is not unusual to run out of words when praying according to our intelligence. Sometimes, our prayer sessions ended out of our limitations to properly express exactly what needed to be communicated to God. There are things we would like to say to God that our human language is incapable of communicating about the will of God. One thing we need not to forget is the fact that Jesus said the Holy Spirit was going to also come in the capacity of a helper to the believer. In his letter to the Romans, Apostle Paul clearly stated the scope and the level of help that the believer is receiving from the Holy Spirit when the believer prays in tongues. He or she receives supernatural reinforcement from the Holy Spirit of God to enable him or her to pray according to the will of God. It is noteworthy to mention that the Bible says in Psalm 138:2 that *"You* (God) *"exalt your word above all your name"* and that He (the Holy Spirit) only acts by what God had already said. In our human limitations, we do not always know how to pray according to the will of God. Here is what Apostle Paul said regarding this:

> *"Likewise the Spirit also helps in our weaknesses. For we do not know what we should pray for as we ought, but the Spirit Himself makes intercession for us with groaning which cannot be uttered. ²⁷ Now He who searches the hearts knows what the mind of the Spirit is because He makes intercession for the saints according to the will of God. (Romans 8:26-27)*

3. - Saying Mysteries

Our common language is a demonstration of our soul expressing itself through our vocal cords. When we pray according to our intelligence, we can understand what we are praying about. People around us can make sense of what we are saying. For most of us, this is the only acceptable way to express ourselves unto God. Nonetheless, we are not left with only one way to express ourselves especially when it comes to communicating with God. In 1 Corinthians 12:31, Apostle Paul offered what he called a more excellent way of communicating with God through tongues.

In times of war, when the opposing party can successfully communicate tactical strategies between ranks without the other party knowing it, victory becomes more probable on one hand. On the other hand, if the opposing party can successfully decode the other party's message, it can strategize a counter-offense to turn the tide in its favor. We believe that our enemy can use our strategies against us sometimes knowing the power of our words. This is where the importance of praying in tongues comes into play. Apostle Paul said *for "he (the believer) who speaks in a tongue does not speak to men but to God, for no one understands him; however, in the spirit, he speaks mysteries" (1 Corinthians 14:2).* The expression no one denotes not only human beings but also spiritual beings.

Just to recap, when praying in tongues, the believer is strategizing against the enemy in a way that no one else but God can understand. The way God answers our prayers made in that manner is an element of surprise to the enemy that strikes definite blows to him. This is the major reason why the enemy has no interest in allowing the church of Jesus Christ to pray in tongues. He prefers negative criticism to discourage the use of speaking in tongues. The opponent will inevitably conquer if he can successfully divide. It is extraordinary to know that the enemy has a better understanding of the power of speaking in tongues than many believers in Jesus Christ. We need to change the tide with the power of the Holy Spirit in our favor. We need to use that weapon until the enemy is left with no place else to hide and nowhere to go in Jesus' name. Amen!

When we pray in tongues, we are communicating directly with God in a way that bypasses our human understanding. That is why we can't understand what we are saying to God unless the Holy Spirit himself gives us the ability to understand what we are saying. Apostle Paul said that we are speaking mysteries in the spirit. We are speaking a language that is impossible to understand or explain. By doing so, we put the enemy in a confusing state because he is unable to make any sense of our conversation with God. This is one more reason why the enemy is trying to decrease our motivation to speak in tongues and to keep as many believers in Jesus Christ as possible away from speaking and praying in tongues. Speaking in tongues is our secret weapon in our spiritual warfare. Neglecting speaking in tongues is to report to the battlefield with no weapons in a battle where the enemy takes no prisoners.

4. - Our spirit prays

In the physical, we all have a name and an address. We can express ourselves in many ways including but not limited to words. Did you know that our spirit also needs to express itself as well? Yes. Your spirit can talk if you let it. The voice of our spirit comes in the form of speaking in tongues. When we speak in tongues, we give our spirit the ability to express itself not in a way that can be physically understood but only God can. Apostle Paul said in 1 Corinthians 14: 14 that *"For if I pray in a tongue, my spirit prays, but my mind is unfruitful."*

Here is a way I look at it. Have you ever been in a situation where you have become more and more frustrated because no one will give you the opportunity to speak or to share the right answers for a better outcome? I believe it is the same when we consider the way that many treat their spirit. Many believers in Jesus Christ has become more and more frustrated and depressed in their lives not knowing what is happening to them. Could it possibly be because their spirit wants to express itself and is prevented to do so through blockages in speaking in tongues?

We must admit that our spirit knows more than our soul does. When we allow our spirit to express itself through tongues, it relays the information directly into our souls. As a result, our soul becomes energized with fresh information that it can get nowhere else. Taking into account the fact that our spirit is sealed with the Holy Spirit, the transfer of data from our spirit is guided by the Holy Spirit. We receive godly insights and directives for our lives and our circumstances.

CHAPTER 11

THE ROLE OF FAITH IN SPEAKING AND PRAYING IN TONGUES

How do we receive baptism with the Holy Spirit? We receive it by asking for it, by believing that we receive it through faith, and then by acting on it by faith. Jesus made that point clearly in the gospel of Luke 11:11-13 when he said the following:

> *"What would you fathers do if your son asks you for a fish? Would any of you give him a snake? Or, if your son asks for an egg, would you give him a scorpion? Even though you are bad, you know how to give good things to your children. So surely your heavenly Father knows how to give the Holy Spirit to those who ask him."*

The Bible teaches us in Hebrews 11:6 that *"Without faith, it is impossible to please God"* and knowing that we are saved by grace through faith underscores the importance of faith in God.

Faith

Generally, having faith involves a three-step process. In the first step, faith is initiated. Faith is initiated when we hear the word of God. In the second step, faith is activated. Faith is activated when we believe in the word we hear from God. It is when we appropriate to ourselves, to our situations, the word we have heard so much so that we start making confessions, declarations, and decrees on the word that we believe. In the third step, faith is demonstrated. At this point, we step out to do what we have already believed in and confessed.

In a nutshell, faith is initiated when we hear the word of God. Faith is activated when we believe in the word of God. Faith is demonstrated when we go all out to move in a direction that is consistent with the word of God we believe in. This is all you will need to speak in tongues and we will lead you through it step by step.

It is important to note that such an experience is available only to those who have repented of their sins and thereby have accepted Jesus Christ in their hearts.

Upon receipt of that baptism, the experience with the Holy Spirit has just started. Ezekiel 47:1-14 points to at least four different possible depths in our relationship with the Holy Spirit. The water in that passage symbolizes the Holy Spirit.

The first depth is called an Ankle deep relationship with the Holy Spirit. This can be best described as a very casual, carefree, and hand-off relationship approach to the Holy Spirit. In this category, are the believers who may not know or may just have a generically broad understanding of the person and ministry of the Holy Spirit in their lives. Knowing more about the Holy Spirit is not a necessity for those believers in that category. The second depth is called a Knee deep relationship with the Holy Spirit. This is described as when the believer accepts to let go of a small portion of their self-reliance to get to know who the Holy Spirit is just a little bit more than they have initially.

The third depth is called a waist-deep relationship with the Holy Spirit. This level describes a deliberate move on the part of the believer to go deeper into his/her understanding of the person and ministry of the Holy Spirit. The fourth depth is one in which the believer is completely submerged into the Holy Spirit to the point that he willingly relinquishes full control of his/her life over to the Holy Spirit. At that level, the Holy Spirit can freely move in his temple unhindered.

CHAPTER 12

ACTIVATION STEPS TO SPEAK AND PRAY IN TONGUES

Have a desire for it.

I had the privilege to work with pregnant mothers for at least ten years. One of the things that I learned is that when they crave something, they will go after it and won't stop until their desires are satisfied. One of my young close female relatives moved from the US to Canada with her family recently. When she got there, she noticed that she was pregnant. She had developed a strong craving for a particular indigenous dish that she could not find or make to her taste in Canada. Four months into that experience, she had decided to move back to the USA solely to enjoy the dish that she was craving until she delivered the baby.

In Psalm 37:4, the believer is encouraged to delight himself or herself in the Lord and thereby will be granted the desires of his or her heart. This is different from a believer who comes to church and sits on the pews saying in his or her heart: *"I am here today. I am not moving to the left nor to the right. I am not going to sing. I am not going to pray and I am not going to read the bible. If anyone can, let him or her come and bless me today"*. That blessing may never come that day or any other day. On the contrary, someone with an attitude to meet God, someone with a hunger to fellowship with God will always leave the service blessed and edified. In order to receive the spiritual gift of speaking in tongues one must have an unquenchable desire for it and it will come to pass.

Ask God to birth the desire for more of him in your heart. This biblical foundation is found in James 1:5 in the following terms: *"If any of you lack wisdom, let him ask of God, that giveth to all men liberally, and upbraided not; and it shall be given him."*

Confession of Sins and Forgiveness to Others

Having the desire, as powerful as it can be is not enough. The believer must conduct a deliberate heart search for unconfessed sins to confess. Grudges against anyone must be put out by the blood of Jesus Christ and forgiveness to others must be the first order of business. We have this powerful hint in many places in the Bible but we will consider what prophet Isaiah had said on that critically important matter in *Isaiah 59:2 "But your iniquities have separated you from your God; your sins have hidden his face from you so that he will not hear"*. In the same line of idea, Jesus said in Matthew 6:15: *"But if you do not forgive others their sins, your Father will not forgive your sins."*

Ask God for it in the name of Jesus

The next step is to ask God to impart upon you the spiritual gift of speaking in tongues. God has no short supply of it. He has more than enough to give to anyone who asks him. Jesus was encouraging his disciples to ask his father. In the process, he made a remarkable point when he said in Luke 11:10-13

> "[10] For everyone who asks receives; he who seeks finds; and to him who knocks, the door will be opened. [11] What father among you, if his son asks for a fish will give him a snake instead? [12] Or if he asks for an egg, will give him a scorpion? [13] So if you who are evil know how to give good gifts to your children, how much

more will your Father in heaven give the Holy Spirit to those who ask Him!"

One of the questions one might have in starting to pray in tongues is who does the speaking? The answer is simple. You do the speaking and the Holy Spirit will allow a flow of words and sounds to come out of your mouth. It requires a little bit of effort in the beginning and faith as you are venturing into an area where you may have not been before. The Holy Spirit will not open your mouth for you to do the speaking. He will cause the words in the form of syllables to come into your mouth and for you to speak them out by faith. Speak as the Holy Spirit gives you utterance.

Your utterance may come in the form of syllables put together at first. It may sound similar to a child whose language articulation is not fully developed. Whatever comes out, speak it out loud with boldness by faith. You will not know what you will be saying but don't worry because God does. Don't stop. If available, use worship instrumental music in the background as loud as you can tolerate it as you speak in your new heavenly language with boldness. Stay at it until you feel something shift on the inside of you. Something will shift in a big or small way. Expect it to happen as you start praying in tongues. Then it will become easier. Keep at it every day as it is your weapon of war against the enemy. The enemy will attempt to discourage you, to make you think that it is not worthwhile. Keep at it. Speak it every day several times a day. Over time, your vocabulary will increase and you will be more and more comfortable doing it.

One of the roadblocks to speaking in tongues is the fact that your mind will not make sense of it. Your mind will fight the sounds coming out of your mouth as nonsense or gibberish. Your mind prefers and thrives to have control over everything that is happening inside of you. In this case, it won't. The good news is what Apostle Paul said in 2 *Corinthians 14:14 "For if I pray in a tongue, my spirit prays but my mind (understanding) is unfruitful"*. In other words, know that there are things your spirit knows that your mind doesn't until your spirit communicates them to your mind. When you pray in tongues, you forcefully silence your mind so that your spirit can have a say in a way that bypasses the mind's micromanagement ambitions. Always remember that persistence breaks resistance every time.

Instructions

It is time now to activate your private prayer language. It is easier than you think. Follow the following simple steps.

1. - Isolate yourself away from any kind of distractions in an attitude of prayer. This is consistent with what Jesus had said in Matthew 6:6 in the following terms: *"But when you pray, go into your room, close the door and pray to your Father, who is unseen. Then your Father, who sees what is done in secret, will reward you"*.

2. - If it is possible, put on some worship instrumental music at a volume that is acceptable to you. Such music has the ability to quiet your soul to allow your spirit to take control.

3. - Close your eyes and focus on Jesus.

Note: Some believers were baptized with the Holy Spirit but waited for days, weeks, months even years to speak in tongues. It ought not to be so. As stated above, whenever this lack of evidence is present, look into the teachings received and the recipient's willingness to move by faith to demonstrate it. It is fine to read this book in part or as a whole over and over again if necessary to attain the level of faith and understanding that is needed to successfully activate your private prayer language.

Prayer of activation

If you are not yet born again, say the following simple prayer with all your heart to accept Jesus in your heart before you can say the tongues activation prayer. The tongue activation prayer is valid only to those who are already born-again believers.

The Sinner's Prayer for Salvation

Say:

Heavenly father,
I declare with my mouth that Jesus is Lord and I believe in my heart that you raised him from the dead. I come to you today to renounce all

sins in my life. Cover me with the blood of Jesus. Change my life. Enter my heart and I promise to live for you from this day forward. In Jesus' name, I pray.

You can receive the spiritual gift of speaking in tongues in one of the following two ways: 1) You can ask a man or woman of God who is already baptized with the Holy Spirit to lay hands on you and to pray for you to receive the baptism with the Holy Spirit or 2) you can do it yourself. Close your eyes and place one hand on your chest and the other one on your head. Then pray the following prayer by faith with an expectation to receive what you are asking for right now in the name of Jesus.

Activation prayer

Lord Jesus,
I surrender myself to you today in a whole new way. Now by faith, I ask that you baptize me with the Holy Spirit with the evidence of speaking in tongues just like it happened on the day of Pentecost. I believe and I receive it by faith in your name. Amen!

If needs be, repeat that prayer over and over again as a faith-building exercise.

After you have prayed by faith, get into action immediately. Open your mouth with faith. Begin to move your tongues with your eyes closed at first. Give voice to what is being stirred in your heart. You will not understand what you are saying. Just cooperate with the Holy Spirit. Stay at it until you feel something shift on the inside of you. Something will shift in a big or small way.

THE LAST WORDS

I pray that this book is a blessing to you. If so, consider sharing it with others. Would you also consider sharing your experience after reading this book? That would help others tremendously in developing their faith in God. If you would like to do so, simply send your testimonies to the following email address: livingw214@gmail.com.

If you feel lead to donate financially in support to this ministry, you can securely do so through either Cash App at: $lwcm2005, through Zelle at: livingw214@gmail.com, or by sending it directly to: 214 Walnut Street, Waterbury CT 06704.

Made in the USA
Middletown, DE
06 September 2024

59899351R00042